A New True Book

EXPERIMENTS WITH STRAWS AND PAPER

By Ray Broekel

CHILDRENS PRESS®

CHICAGO

Did you ever drink out
of a straw like this?

PHOTO CREDITS

© Cameramann International, Ltd.—Cover, 2, 4, 7, 8, 9,
10, 11, 12, 13 (4 photos), 15, 16, 17 (2 photos), 18,
19, 20, 21, 24, 25, 26 (2 photos), 29, 30, 31
(2 photos), 32 (2 photos), 33, 34, 36, 37, 39, 40, 42,
43, 44, 45

Charles Hills—23

Cover: Child with straws and paper

. Library of Congress Cataloging-in-Publication Data

Broekel, Ray.
  Experiments with straws and paper / by Ray Broekel.
    p.   cm. — (A New true book)
  Includes index.
  Summary: Illustrates some basic principles of
science, based on experiments and tricks using straws,
paper, drinking glasses, and coins.
  IBSN 0-516-01104-9
  1. Science—Experiments—Juvenile literature.
[1. Science—Experiments. 2. Experiments.]
I. Title. II. Series.
Q164.B832 1990   90-2173
962—dc20   CIP
                                       AC

TABLE OF CONTENTS

INTRODUCTION

Science can be mysterious. Science can be magical. But when we begin to understand why things happen the way they do, science can be fun.

Let's do a few experiments and have some fun with science.

DRINKING STRAWS

A drinking straw is a tube used to suck up liquids. Today, straws are made of paper, plastic, or glass. But long ago, the dried stems of grains or other grasslike plants were used as straws.

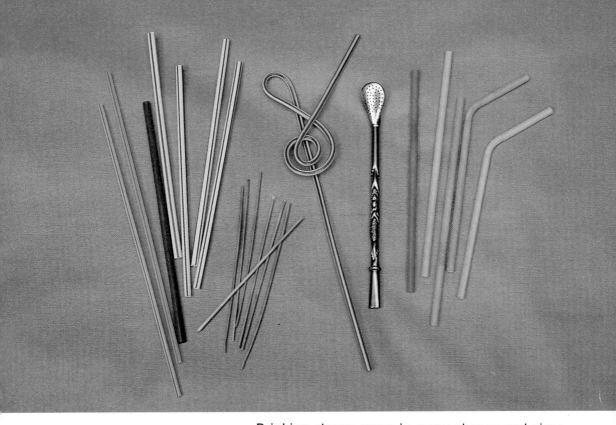

Drinking straws come in many shapes and sizes.

If someone asked you
what was inside a straw,
would you say, "Nothing"?
But there *is* something
inside a straw. It is air. Air
is everywhere around us.

There *is* something inside the straw!

We can't see it or feel it,
but it is there.
The following experiments
will show you how air works.

MOVING MILK WITH A STRAW

The milk stays in the straw.

EXPERIMENT

Equipment: 1 straw
1 glass
half full
of milk

Do you know how to move milk out of a glass without using your mouth, or without pouring the milk out? First, put the straw into the glass of milk. The milk will rise up in the straw.

Now put your finger over the top of the straw and lift the straw out of the glass. You'll see that you lifted the milk in the straw out of the glass too.

9

Now
the milk
flows out.

You did this because your finger cut off the outside air that was pushing down on the inside of the straw. When you lifted the straw out of the milk, the air pressure pushed up at the bottom of the straw. That air pressure kept the milk in the straw.

When you take your finger off the top of the straw, the milk flows out. Why? Because air pressure can once again push down inside the straw.

THE MYSTERY STRAWS

EXPERIMENT

Equipment: 2 straws
             1 glass half full of milk

First, put one straw inside the glass. Then, holding the other straw outside the glass, put the two ends in your mouth. Now try to drink milk from the glass.

What happens? Do you know why the lighter air from the straw outside the glass was drawn into your mouth rather than the

heavier milk? Can you figure out how to drink milk from the glass? Try putting your tongue over the top of the straw that is outside the glass. Now can you suck up the milk? Do you know why?

When you suck on a straw, you reduce the air pressure in the straw. Because the air pressure on the surface of the milk in the glass has not been reduced, it forces milk up inside the straw!

PAPER

Paper is made mainly of wood pulp and rags. It is used for many tasks, such as writing and wrapping things.

We can also use paper to show how certain principles of science work.

Books are printed on paper, and people use paper to do artwork.

KEEPING THE PAPER DRY

EXPERIMENT

Equipment: paper (8½"x11")
              1 glass
              1 clear plastic container

Can you put paper into water without getting it wet?

Crumple up the paper and jam it tightly into the bottom of the glass. Then fill the clear plastic container about half full of water.

Now turn the glass upside down. Push it into the water in the container. Be sure to keep the glass straight as you push down.

The paper inside the glass does not get wet!

This happens because there was air in the glass as well as paper. Air takes up space. When you push a glass full of air and paper into water, the air inside the glass keeps the water out of the glass.

This experiment is one way of showing that air takes up space.

PAPER CAN HOLD WATER IN

EXPERIMENT

Equipment: 1 glass of water
                   1 index card (3"x 5")
Do this experiment at the kitchen sink.

Fill the glass with water. Then place the index card on top of the glass. Make certain the index card covers the opening of the glass completely.

Now hold the card firmly in place with your hand and quickly turn the glass upside down. Be careful. Do not let any bubbles of air get between the card and the glass as you are turning it upside down.

Now gently remove your hand from below the card. Do not jiggle the glass or the card.

The card holds the water in the glass!

Do you know why the water in the glass does not run out and push the card off?

The water is held inside the glass by air pressure. The pressure of the air outside the glass against the card is greater than the pressure of the water inside the glass against the card.

IS PAPER STRONG?

Do you think paper can hold up something that is much heavier than the paper itself?

EXPERIMENT

Equipment: 1 rubber band
            paper (8½"x11")
            small paperback book

First, roll the paper into a cylinder or tube, put the rubber band around it and stand it up carefully on a table. Then balance the book on top of the cylinder of paper. The paper is strong enough to hold up the book!

Paper and other materials are much stronger when they are rolled into a cylinder. The cylinder form is often used in building because it is so strong.

PAPER AND PLANES

What makes a plane
rise off the ground? You
can do the experiment on
the next page to find out.

Airplanes can fly even though they are heavier than air.

MOVING THE PAPER

EXPERIMENT

Equipment: paper (8½"x11")
            2 books

First, place the books about three inches apart on a table. Then place the paper on the books so that it covers the space between them.

Now blow as hard as you can *under* the paper covering the space. Does it blow away? Why not?

The air from your mouth speeds up as it enters the space beneath the paper. Because the air under the paper has speeded up, the air pressure under the paper is less than the air pressure above the paper. The paper is pressed down by the heavier air from above and so it does not blow away.

A Swiss scientist named Daniel Bernoulli discovered that fast-moving gases (such as air) and fast-moving liquids have less pressure than slower-moving gases and liquids. The upper part of an airplane wing is curved. This means that air has to move faster and farther over the wing than under it.

Because the air on top of the wing moves faster, there is less air pressure on top of the wing than under the wing.

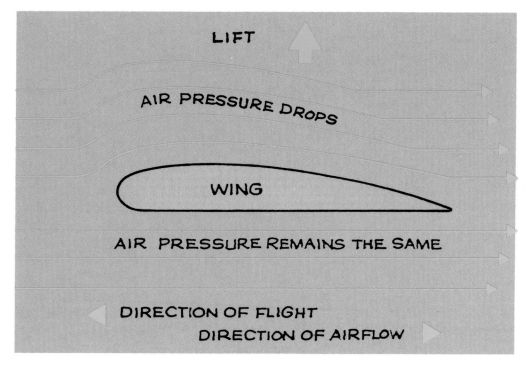

This airplane is just beginning to rise into the air.

So, as a plane moves
along the runway, it
gathers speed. There is
then less air pressure on
top of the wing and the
plane rises off the ground.

INERTIA

A property that scientists call *inertia* can be seen in the following experiments.

COIN DROP EXPERIMENT

Equipment: 1 index card   1 coin
             1 glass

Can you drop a coin into a glass without touching the coin?

First, put the index card on top of the glass.

25

You may have to do this experiment several times before you get it right.

Then put the coin on top of the index card.

To make the coin drop, give the card a quick snap with your finger. Touch only the index card.

Why did the coin drop? Inertia will keep the coin still if the card is flipped from beneath it quickly. The coin's inertia makes it fall into the glass, rather than go with the card as it is flipped.

26

There are two kinds of inertia—inertia of rest and inertia of motion. Inertia of rest is the tendency of an object that is not moving to remain still unless some force acts on the object.

Inertia of motion is the tendency of an object that is moving to keep moving

at the same speed and in
the same direction unless
a force acts on the object.

The inertia of rest
affecting the coin on top
of the card caused it to
fall into the glass when
the card was moved.

Have you ever
experienced inertia? You
may experience inertia

when you are in a bus or a car. If the driver starts up suddenly, the bodies of the people inside move back because their bodies are in a state of inertia of rest.

A sudden stop makes the riders lean forward.

When the driver
suddenly stops, the bodies
of the people move
forward because their
bodies are in a state of
inertia of motion.

INERTIA EXPERIMENT

EXPERIMENT

Equipment: 1 glass
                   1 marble

    First, place the glass on its side on a table.
Put it near the edge of the table with the open
end pointing toward the center of the table.
    Then put the marble about halfway into the
glass. Now push the glass forward on the
table.

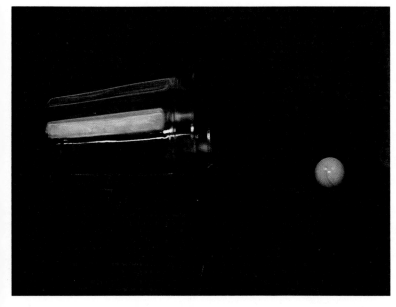
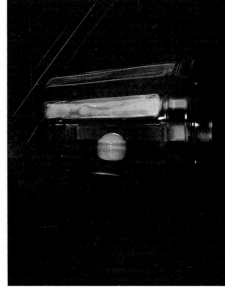

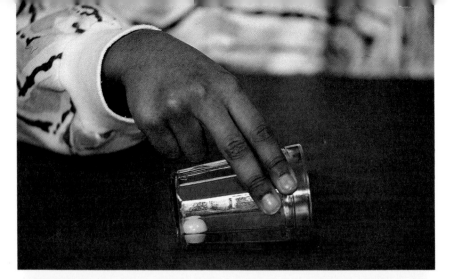

Top: inertia of rest keeps the marble from moving.
Bottom: inertia of motion keeps the marble from stopping.

What happens to the marble? Does it shoot out of the glass? No, it stays in the glass. The marble in the moving glass is in a state of inertia of rest.

But what happens when you suddenly stop moving the glass? The marble rolls out! The rolling marble shows the inertia of motion.

INERTIA AND PAPER

Here's another way to show inertia.

EXPERIMENT

Equipment: 1 sheet of newspaper.

First, hold the newspaper in one hand so that it drops down in front of you. Then *slowly* push against the paper with your finger. The paper will move as you push it, but that's all. Your finger will not go through the paper.

You would have to move your finger very quickly to pierce the paper!

The paper moves away from a slowly moving finger.

A quick, sharp jab of the finger will rip the paper.

Because of inertia, the air on both sides of the paper resists any movement for a short time. If you move your finger *quickly*, the paper will tear because the air behind the paper resists the force of your finger.

But, if you move your finger *slowly*, there is time for the pressure of your finger to overcome the resistance of the air. So the whole sheet of paper is pushed out. Inertia strikes again!

RIGHT-EYED
OR LEFT-EYED?

Which hand do you use most? Are you left-handed or right-handed? Do you know which of your eyes is the dominant or stronger eye?

You can find out which is your dominant eye by doing the following experiment.

Is your dominant eye on the same side as your dominant hand?

EXPERIMENT

First, stand and point with your right forefinger at something about ten feet away. Keep both eyes open and look at your forefinger. Now shut your right eye.

If your right eye is the dominant one, your forefinger will seem to jump. If your left eye is dominant, your finger won't move.

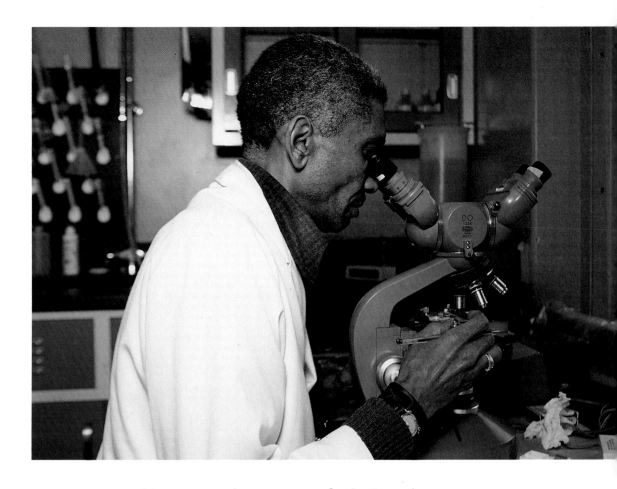

It can be useful to know
which eye is dominant. For
one thing, you can see
better through a telescope
or microscope using your
dominant eye.

THE "HOLE" TRUTH

Can you see through a hole in your hand? Would you like to try?

EXPERIMENT

Equipment: 1 large sheet of paper

First, roll the sheet of paper into a tube. Hold the tube up to your right eye, close your left eye, and look through the tube.

Hold your left palm toward you, against the left side of the tube. Open your left eye. Do you see a hole in your left hand?

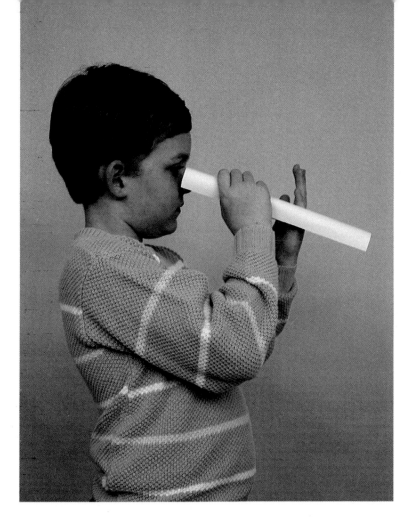

When the separate images from your two eyes join together, the image of the hole overlaps the image of the hand.

This happens because your eyes are seeing two different things. Your right eye is seeing through the tube. But your left eye doesn't see the same thing because its view is blocked by your left hand.

So a hole seems to appear in your left hand. This is called an illusion. It happens because your two eyes normally produce a single image.

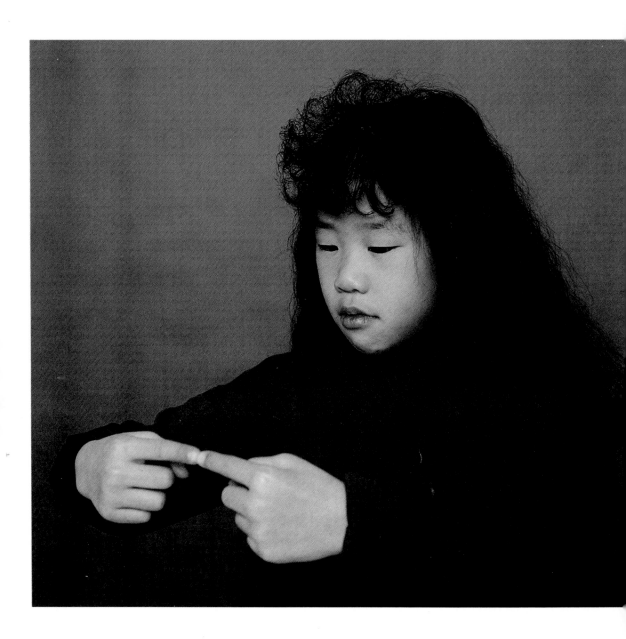

AN "EXTRA" BIT OF FINGER

EXPERIMENT

Touch the forefingers of each hand together about twelve inches in front of you. Focus your eyes at the tips of the two fingers.

Now focus your eyes on a distant wall. What happens? An "extra" bit of finger appears between your fingertips!

Where did this "extra" bit come from? It was made by your eyes when you tried to make them do two things at the same time.

As you looked past your fingers at the wall, each eye made a separate, side-by-side image of your fingers. These images overlapped at the center. That's why there seemed to be an "extra" bit of finger.

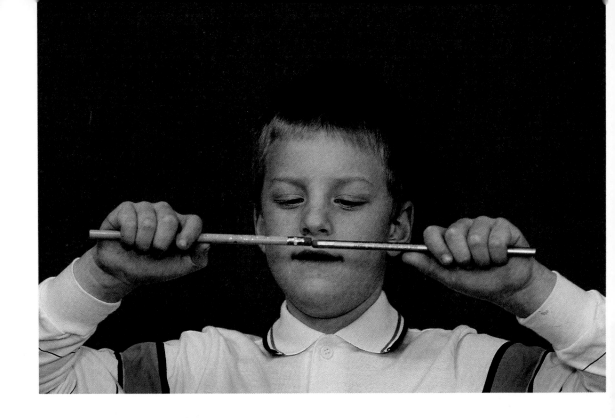

TWO EYES ARE BETTER THAN ONE

EXPERIMENT

Equipment: 2 pencils

Hold the pencils at arm's length with the eraser ends facing each other. Keep them about two feet apart.

With both eyes open, bring the eraser ends together so that they touch. Do this several times. That was easy, right?

Now close one eye and try to bring the eraser ends together again. What happened?

Why is it hard to make the two eraser ends meet with one eye closed? Because two eyes are better than one—especially in estimating direction.

Do the eraser ends come closer to touching if your dominant eye is open?

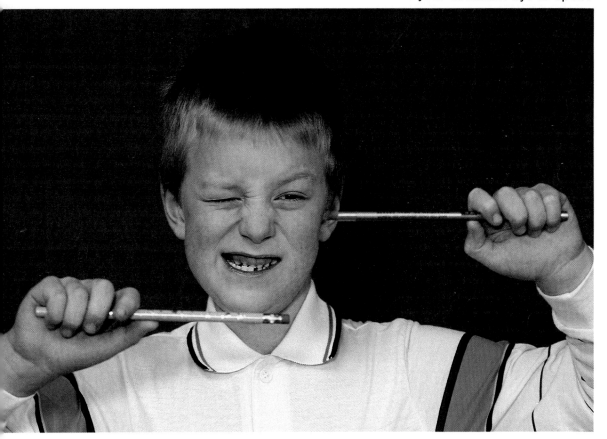

YOUR BLIND SPOT

EXPERIMENT

First, make a cross and a circle on an index card. Put the circle on the right and put the cross about three inches to the left of the circle.

Now close your right eye and hold the card at arm's length. Look at the circle as you move the card slowly toward you.

The cross will disappear as you continue to look at the circle. Why?

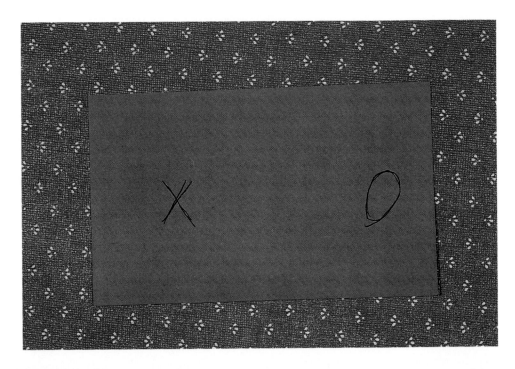

The cross will reappear if you keep
moving the card toward you.

This happens because each of us has a
blind spot. The point at which the optic nerve
joins the retina of the eye is insensitive to
light. So light falling on this point does not
produce an image. You've found your blind
spot!

We hope you've had fun
doing the experiments in
this book. Science can
indeed be mysterious until
you know the answers.

WORDS YOU SHOULD KNOW

air pressure (AYR PRESH•er) — the force of air against an object

blind spot (BLYND SPAHT) — a small spot at the back of the eyeball where the optic nerve enters the eye

cylinder (SILL•in•der) — a round tube bounded by two flat ends that are parallel circles

dominant (DAHM•ih•nint) — most important; most powerful

focus (FOH•kuss) — to adjust the eyes to produce a clear image

gas (GAS) — a substance that is not solid or liquid, but is fluid and able to expand indefinitely

illusion (il•LOO•zhun) — a deceiving appearance or the false impression it gives

image (IM•ije) — an exact likeness of an object

inertia (in•ER•sha) — the continuance of an object in its particular state of rest or motion unless it is acted upon by some force

liquid (LICK•wid) — a substance that flows more or less freely and may be poured from its container; a fluid that is not a gas

optic nerve (AHP•tik NERV) — the nerve that carries the sensation of seeing from the eye to the brain

paper (PAY•per) — a material made mainly from wood pulp and rags

retina (REH•tih•na) — the layer of cells at the back of the eyeball that are sensitive to light

straw (STRAW) — a thin tube that is usually made of plastic, glass, or paper, and used to suck up a liquid

INDEX

About the Author

Ray Broekel is well known in the publishing field as a teacher, editor, and author of science materials for young people. Today, Dr. Broekel is still having fun doing science experiments with his grandchildren.

Dr. Broekel has had over 200 books published. They are in many areas, and some are written for adults. He is an authority on candy bar and chocolate history, and has written several books and many articles on those subjects.

His first book was published by Childrens Press in 1956. He now lives with his wife, Peg, and dog, BB, in Ipswich, Massachusetts.